FOUNDATIONS OF DEMOCRACY

EMPLOYMENT AND WORKERS' RIGHTS

FOUNDATIONS OF DEMOCRACY

Citizenship and Immigration

Corruption and Transparency

Employment and Workers' Rights

Gender Equality and Identity Rights

Justice, Policing, and the Rule of Law

Political Participation and Voting Rights

Religious, Cultural, and Minority Rights

Speech, Media, and Protest

Foundations of Democracy

Employment and Workers' Rights

Jack Covarubias and Tom Lansford

Series Advisor: Tom Lansford
Professor of Political Science
University of Southern Mississippi, Gulf Coast

MASON CREST

Mason Crest
450 Parkway Drive, Suite D
Broomall, PA 19008
www.masoncrest.com

© 2017 by Mason Crest, an imprint of National Highlights, Inc. All rights reserved. No part of this publication may be reproduced or transmitted in any form or by any means, electronic or mechanical, including photocopying, recording, taping, or any information storage and retrieval system, without permission from the publisher.

MTM Publishing, Inc.
435 West 23rd Street, #8C
New York, NY 10011
www.mtmpublishing.com

President: Valerie Tomaselli
Vice President, Book Development: Hilary Poole
Designer: Annemarie Redmond
Copyeditor: Peter Jaskowiak
Editorial Assistant: Andrea St. Aubin

Series ISBN: 978-1-4222-3625-3
Hardback ISBN: 978-1-4222-3628-4
E-Book ISBN: 978-1-4222-8272-4

Cataloging-in-Publication Data on file with the Library of Congress

Printed and bound in the United States of America.

First printing
9 8 7 6 5 4 3 2 1

TABLE OF CONTENTS

Series Introduction.. 7
Chapter One: Evolution of Workers' Rights 9
Chapter Two: Unions and Collective Action 19
Chapter Three: Working Conditions 29
Chapter Four: Fairness in the Workplace 39
Chapter Five: Termination 48
Further Reading 57
Series Glossary 58
Index 60
About the Author 64
About the Advisor 64
Photo Credits 64

Key Icons to Look for:

Words to Understand: These words with their easy-to-understand definitions will increase the reader's understanding of the text, while building vocabulary skills.

Sidebars: This boxed material within the main text allows readers to build knowledge, gain insights, explore possibilities, and broaden their perspectives by weaving together additional information to provide realistic and holistic perspectives.

Research Projects: Readers are pointed toward areas of further inquiry connected to each chapter. Suggestions are provided for projects that encourage deeper research and analysis.

Text-Dependent Questions: These questions send the reader back to the text for more careful attention to the evidence presented there.

Series Glossary of Key Terms: This back-of-the-book glossary contains terminology used throughout the series. Words found here increase the reader's ability to read and comprehend higher-level books and articles in this field.

Iraqi women at a political rally in 2010, in advance of the country's parliamentary elections.

SERIES INTRODUCTION

Democracy is a form of government in which the people hold all or most of the political power. In democracies, government officials are expected to take actions and implement policies that reflect the will of the majority of the citizenry. In other political systems, the rulers generally rule for their own benefit, or at least they usually put their own interests first. This results in deep differences between the rulers and the average citizen. In undemocratic states, elites enjoy far more privileges and advantages than the average citizen. Indeed, autocratic governments are often created to exploit the average citizen.

Elections allow citizens to choose representatives to make choices for them, and under some circumstances to decide major issues themselves. Yet democracy is much more than campaigns and elections. Many nations conduct elections but are not democratic. True democracy is dependent on a range of freedoms for its citizenry, and it simultaneously exists to protect and enhance those freedoms. At its best, democracy ensures that elites, average citizens, and even groups on the margins of society all have the same rights, privileges, and opportunities. The components of democracy have changed over time as individuals and groups have struggled to expand equality. In doing so, the very notion of what makes up a democracy has evolved. The volumes in this series examine the core freedoms that form the foundation of modern democracy.

Citizenship and Immigration explores what it means to be a citizen in a democracy. The principles of democracy are based on equality, liberty, and government by the consent of the people. Equality means that all citizens have the same rights and responsibilities. Democracies have struggled to integrate all groups and ensure full equality. Citizenship in a democracy is the formal recognition that a person is a member of the country's political community. Modern democracies have faced profound debates over immigration, especially how many people to admit to the country and what rights to confer on immigrants who are not citizens.

Challenges have also emerged within democracies over how to ensure disadvantaged groups enjoy full equality with the majority, or traditionally dominant, populations. While outdated legal or political barriers have been mostly removed, democracies still struggle to overcome cultural or economic impediments to equality. *Gender Equality and Identity Rights* analyzes why gender equality has proven especially challenging, requiring political, economic, and cultural reforms. Concurrently, *Religious, Cultural, and Minority Rights* surveys the efforts that democracies have undertaken to integrate disadvantaged groups into the political, economic, and social mainstream.

A free and unfettered media provides an important check on government power and ensures an informed citizenry. The importance of free expression and a free press are detailed in *Speech, Media, and Protest,* while *Employment and Workers' Rights* provides readers with an overview of the importance of economic liberty and the ways in which employment and workers' rights reinforce equality by guaranteeing opportunity.

The maintenance of both liberty and equality requires a legal system in which the police are constrained by the rule of law. This means that security officials understand and respect the rights of individuals and groups and use their power in a manner that benefits communities, not represses them. While this is the ideal, legal systems continue to struggle to achieve equality, especially among disadvantaged groups. These topics form the core of *Justice, Policing, and the Rule of Law.*

Corruption and Transparency examines the greatest danger to democracy: corruption. Corruption can undermine people's faith in government and erode equality. Transparency, or open government, provides the best means to prevent corruption by ensuring that the decisions and actions of officials are easily understood.

As discussed in *Political Participation and Voting Rights,* a government of the people requires its citizens to provide regular input on policies and decisions through consultations and voting. Despite the importance of voting, the history of democracies has been marked by the struggle to expand voting rights. Many groups, including women, only gained the right to vote in the last century, and continue to be underrepresented in political office.

Ultimately, all of the foundations of democracy are interrelated. Equality ensures liberty, while liberty helps maintain equality. Meanwhile, both are necessary for a government by consent to be effective and lasting. Within a democracy, all people must be treated equally and be able to enjoy the full range of liberties of the country, including rights such as free speech, religion, and voting.

—Tom Lansford

Chapter One

EVOLUTION OF WORKERS' RIGHTS

Words to Understand

anarchist: a person who believes that government should be abolished because it enslaves or otherwise represses people.

Industrial Revolution: a period of rapid change in the late 1700s and early 1800s, marked by technological innovation, the expansion of manufacturing, and growing urbanization.

socialist: describes a political system in which major businesses or industries are owned or regulated by the community instead of by individuals or privately owned companies.

strike: a labor stoppage by workers, used in an effort to improve working conditions or to protest mistreatment by employers.

trade union: an organizations of workers within a specific economic field, or trade, that promotes better employment conditions, wages, and benefits for its members.

transportation: the forced relocation, often permanent, for those accused of crimes.

EMPLOYMENT AND WORKERS' RIGHTS

For most of human history, workers have had few if any rights. The majority of people were farmers or agricultural workers who were employed by large landowners. Until the **Industrial Revolution** began in Europe in the 1700s, as many as 90 percent of people worked in agriculture. There was a small population of skilled artisans in Europe who often banded together in towns and cities to create guilds, or professional societies. The guilds developed training or apprenticeship programs for new members and set rules and regulations for members on prices, wages, and working conditions. They were elitist groups with limited membership—often, they were open only to sons of existing guild members. It was therefore difficult for the average person to gain membership in a guild.

"The Governors of the Haarlem Guild of St. Luke" (1675), by Jan de Bray. The guild had painters and craftsmen of all kinds as members.

CHAPTER ONE: EVOLUTION OF WORKERS' RIGHTS

By the 1700s, the guilds began to be superseded by **trade unions**, which sought to represent not just highly skilled workers, but all employees within a particular economic sector. Unions emerged in reaction to the Industrial Revolution, which saw both a dramatic expansion of nonfarm workers and a deterioration in working conditions. Unions would emerge as the primary advocates for employment rights over the next century.

Working Conditions of the Industrial Revolution

New tools and agricultural techniques led to a dramatic increase in population in Europe from the 1600s to the 1900s. For example, in Great Britain, the population rose from 5.5 million in 1700, to more than 9 million a century later. This led to an excess of workers, many of whom traveled to urban areas in search of work. Since so many people were seeking employment, employers were able to pay them less and require longer working hours. Factory employees often worked 14–16 hours per day, six to six-and-a-half days per week. Women usually were paid half (or even less) of the wages earned by men, while children as young as six were commonly employed, earning about one-tenth what adults made. Workers often faced deductions for food, clothing, or tools supplied by the factory. The work was hard and often dangerous. Workers who were injured or sick for an extended period were often simply dismissed and replaced.

The main tactic used to fight for higher wages and better working conditions was the **strike**. By withholding their labor, workers could stop the production of goods or the completion of services. This would cause business owners to lose profits and suffer other economic woes, ranging from lost customers to wasted supplies. The effectiveness of strikes led business owners and elites to support laws that prohibited labor shortages. For instance, Great Britain enacted the Combination Acts in 1799 and 1800, which banned labor strikes (these were repealed in 1824).

EMPLOYMENT AND WORKERS' RIGHTS

 ## INDUSTRIAL REVOLUTION

The Industrial Revolution in Western Europe and North America led to dramatic innovations in technology that permanently changed working conditions.

In 1764, for instance, the spinning jenny was invented. The machine allowed workers to make more than one spool of thread at a time. Within 15 years, there were more than 22,000 spinning jennys being used in Great Britain. There were other innovations in textiles and iron production, but one of the most significant advances was the invention of the steam engine by Thomas Newcomen in 1712, with later improvements made in the 1760s and 1770s by James Watt. The steam engine revolutionized manufacturing and transportation. The use of the steam engine in railroads and boats dramatically increased the speed and reliability by which supplies and goods could be delivered. The invention of the telegraph in 1837 would also significantly speed up communications. These new technologies meant that some skilled artisans were replaced by machines, while working conditions and worker safety dramatically declined.

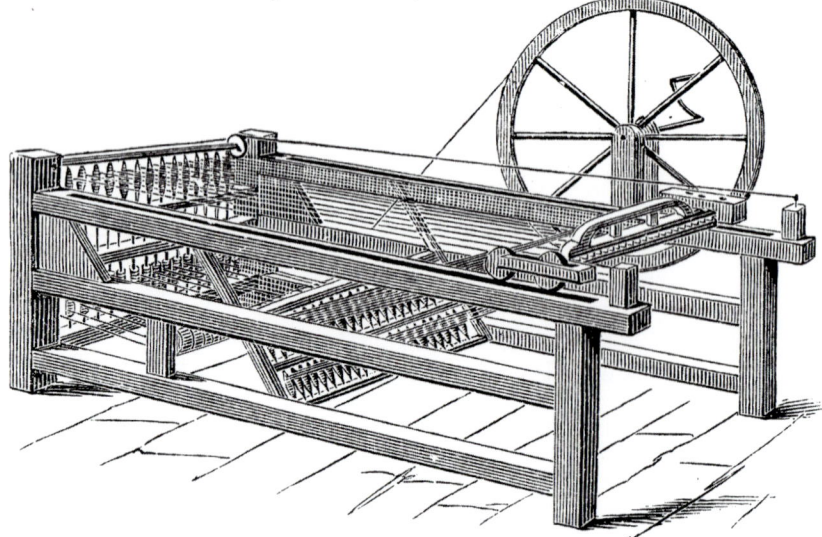

An illustration of a spinning jenny created by the inventor James Hargreaves.

CHAPTER ONE: EVOLUTION OF WORKERS' RIGHTS

Labor Unrest

Disputes between laborers and employers often resulted in violence. In Great Britain in the early 19th century, textile workers and weavers were distressed by the increasing use of machines in their trade. Workers in Great Britain who came to be known as "Luddites" intentionally destroyed machinery in protest of industrialization and the concurrent loss of wages and employment. The term *Luddite* has come to mean anyone who is opposed to new technology.

In response to a series of raids and riots that destroyed industrial machinery and factories, the government passed the Frame Breaking Act of 1812, which made destroying machinery an offense punishable by execution. But in practice, forced **transportation** to Australia was a more common punishment. Transportation was a common practice among imperial powers during the 1700s and 1800s as a means to reduce prison populations and increase the number of settlers in colonies.

In 1834, French workers in Lyon went on strike when factory owners tried to lower wages. The government deployed troops, killing somewhere between 100 and 400 protestors. In addition, several thousand workers were arrested and sentenced to long prison terms or transportation to French colonies. Protests on behalf of economic and political reforms led to a wave of revolutions throughout Europe in 1848.

In the United States, a widespread railroad strike in 1877 led to riots and shut down rail traffic across the nation. President Rutherford B. Hayes deployed troops who brutally suppressed the strikers. On July 14, 1877, police fought strikers in what came to be called the Battle of the Viaduct. Approximately 30 strikers were killed, and more than 100 injured, while 13 police were wounded.

On May 4, 1886, in Haymarket Square, Chicago, during a demonstration in support of striking workers, a bomb was thrown at police who were trying to suppress the protestors. After the explosion, police opened fire on the demonstrators. Seven police officers were killed and 60 injured in the bomb blast and the subsequent violence. Meanwhile, 4 protestors were killed, along with more than 70 wounded. Over 100 protestors were arrested.

EMPLOYMENT AND WORKERS' RIGHTS

Eight prominent labor activists and **anarchists** were arrested and convicted for conspiracy in connection with the Haymarket Riot, although no one was ever charged with actually throwing the explosive. One of the eight committed suicide in prison, four others were hanged, and the remainder were pardoned. The police were subsequently criticized for overreacting and firing on the crowd, while many argued that the four hanged men were innocent. The episode initially led to a loss of support for unions and workers' rights, but over time the incident galvanized labor groups and helped lead to the establishment of May Day (May 1) as an international labor holiday.

LABOR REFORMS

Rising violence and growing sentiment that economic reforms were needed led governments to pass a series of measures in the late 1800s and early 1900s that defined the modern conception of workers' rights. One of the central demands of workers was a reduction in the workday from the 14 or 16 hours common in the 1700s. In 1848, France cut the workday to 12 hours. In 1856, Australia initiated the 8-hour workday for certain skilled laborers, including stonemasons; the 8-hour workday was expanded to all professions in the 1920s. In the United States, the 8-hour workday was instituted in 1916 for railroad workers, but others did not gain the reduction until the 1930s and 1940s.

Reformers also won restrictions on child labor. As early as 1841, France banned child labor in factories before the age of 8. In 1938, the United States prohibited employing children under 16 in dangerous occupations such as mining or manufacturing. Additional rules were put in place in 1949. Often, these measures also included efforts to regulate the safety of the workplace. For instance, an 1872 British law mandated the use of a number of safety precautions for miners. French laws of the same period regulated the use of dangerous chemicals in manufacturing and set minimum hygiene standards in company kitchens and restrooms.

CHAPTER ONE: EVOLUTION OF WORKERS' RIGHTS

From Harper's Weekly, an illustration of violent confrontations between soldiers and strikers during the Great Railroad Strike of 1877.

EMPLOYMENT AND WORKERS' RIGHTS

A poster from the National Child Labor Committee, circa 1910, highlights the dangers of child labor.

Another major labor reform was the minimum wage, which required that all workers be paid at least a certain amount. New Zealand enacted the first national minimum wage in 1894, followed by Australia, two years later. The first national

CHAPTER ONE: EVOLUTION OF WORKERS' RIGHTS

 ## WORKERS' POLITICAL PARTIES

As workers increasing sought to assert their rights in the late 1800s, labor groups began to form political parties to enact new laws and policies to protect those rights. In Great Britain, in 1893, the Labour Party was formed to promote workers' rights. It grew quickly in size and power. In 1900 only 2 members of the Labour Party were elected to Parliament, but six years later that number rose to 29. Today, the Labour Party is one of the two main political parties in Great Britain (although it has significantly broadened its focus beyond workers' rights).

Across industrializing countries, numerous **socialist** parties and organizations emerged. These groups argued that the government should own major industries, in the belief that wages and working conditions would be better than those experienced under private ownership. In 1864, the International Workingman's Association (known simply as the First International) was founded in an effort to promote socialism and unite workers around the world. Groups such as the First International played an important role in antigovernment movements, especially in countries such as France, Germany, and Russia.

Supporters of the Labour Party at a demonstration.

17

EMPLOYMENT AND WORKERS' RIGHTS

minimum wage in the United States was established in 1938. It set the lowest permissible wage at 25 cents an hour.

These types of reforms served as the cornerstone for contemporary labor law. They redefined the relationship between worker and employer by giving laborers a series of basic rights and protections. They also authorized governments to intervene to protect workers.

Text-Dependent Questions

1. Why did trade unions supersede guilds?
2. What was the main tactic used by unions to gain concessions from employers? Why did it work?
3. What types of labor reforms were initiated by governments in the late 1800s and early 1900s?

Research Projects

1. Research the Industrial Revolution and write a report on working conditions in a particular industry, such as textiles, mining, or iron production.
2. Research child labor during the 1800s. Write a report that explores what life was like for most child workers. What were their wages? What were their hours? What were working conditions like?

Chapter Two

UNIONS AND COLLECTIVE ACTION

Words to Understand

arbitration: the use of a neutral third party, the arbitrator, to settle disputes between two sides; the decision of the arbitrator is final and binding on the two parties in disagreement.

collective bargaining: the ability of a workers' organization, such as a union, to negotiate on behalf of its members on issues such as working conditions, wages, and retirement.

labor board: a government body that oversees union organization, certifies union elections, and investigates working conditions.

lockout: the partial or full closure of a business by management or owners in an effort to secure concessions from workers.

picket: a form of protest whereby workers and their supporters attempt to persuade or prevent customers or fellow employees from entering a business.

right-to-work laws: laws in the United States that forbid union membership as a condition for employment.

EMPLOYMENT AND WORKERS' RIGHTS

As noted in the previous chapter, unions played an integral role in the struggle to secure workers' rights. However, unions or organized labor often faced persecution and suppression. Some countries banned traditional unions, and those bans continue today in some cases, such as in China, Cuba, and Saudi Arabia. This is especially significant because China had the world's second-largest economy in 2015. (See sidebar on page 21 for a discussion of China's version of a union.)

This label from the early 20th century was placed on products to certify that the item was made in a factory unionized by the American Federation of Labor.

CHAPTER TWO: UNIONS AND COLLECTIVE ACTION

THE ALL-CHINA FEDERATION OF TRADE UNIONS

The largest union in the world is the All-China Federation of Trade Unions (ACFTU), a collection of industry-specific groups and regional organizations. It has more than 130 million members. The ACFTU was established in 1925, but it was restricted and then banned in 1966. It was reestablished 12 years later under the control of the Chinese Communist Party.

Although it is called a union, the ACFTU does not have the same rights or powers of unions in democratic states. It cannot strike without permission from the government. In addition, the members of the organization cannot elect their leaders, and employers do not have to negotiate through collective bargaining with employees. Meanwhile, workers cannot form other unions without the permission of the government.

The right to form unions emerged as a central component of workers' rights. In modern democracies, unions are common, although they have different powers or roles depending on the country. In some instances, unions are controversial. Corruption has been problematic at times. Some union leaders have used their power to enrich themselves and their supporters at the expense of their membership. In addition, unions have sometimes assumed a political role that does not necessarily reflect the core mission of advancing the welfare and working conditions of their members. Nonetheless, the ability to form unions remains a key component of workers' rights in contemporary democracies.

Union Formation and Right-to-Work Laws

Unions can be a powerful tool for workers to achieve higher wages or better benefits. Consequently, some business owners and corporations try to prevent employees from unionizing in order to save money on wages and to maintain more control over working conditions. Although there are some minor differences, most democracies have very similar laws on union organization.

Employees must indicate their desire for a union, usually through pledge cards or other forms that indicate a preference for union membership. The membership cards are used to petition either a local or national **labor board** regarding the need to hold an election to form a new union or to become part of an existing organization. If the majority of employees vote for a union, then that paves the way for its formation. Some

Members of the United Auto Workers union gather outside the Ford Motor Company's River Rouge factory in 1937. The situation escalated when union organizers were physically attacked by company security guards in what became known as the "Battle of the Overpass."

CHAPTER TWO: UNIONS AND COLLECTIVE ACTION

UNION CORRUPTION

Unions collect dues from their workers and can sometimes have poor oversight of how that money is spent. In addition, unscrupulous union leaders have sometimes used their positions to seek bribes or other payments from companies with which the unions do business. In the United States, the Department of Labor investigates about 100 cases of corruption within unions each year. For instance, in 2008 it was found that the heads of a branch of the Amalgamated Transit Union in New York (the union of school bus drivers) had arranged an illicit deal with four school bus inspectors. The inspectors received bribes from bus companies in exchange for easier inspections of vehicles and contracts with the union.

nations specify a minimum number of workers in order for a union to be established. In India, for example, there must be at least seven employees eligible for membership to establish a union.

Once a union is either formed or approved by workers, and certified by a government labor board, the management of a business must recognize the union and negotiate with it on a labor contract. Once a contract is finalized, it must be approved by a majority of union members at the business.

Unions depend on their members for dues, which keep the organizations operating and pay for legal fees and other costs. However, unions also use dues to contribute to political candidates and support other political activities, a practice some workers may oppose. Some businesses are known as "open shop," which means that an employee does not have to join a union to work at the facility. In contrast, "closed shop" companies require an employee to be a member of a union in order to work there. In the United States, in some areas, **right-to-work laws** prohibit closed-shop arrangements and forbid requirements for workers to join unions. Opponents of these laws assert that they weaken unions and are not fair, since unions negotiate for the benefit of all workers, but under this arrangement they receive dues and support from only those in open shops. By 2015, 25 U.S. states had right-to-work laws. In other countries, closed shops (also known as "union shops") are strictly illegal, including Australia, New Zealand, and the United Kingdom.

Collective Bargaining

Central to the power and influence of unions is **collective bargaining**, which allows organized labor to negotiate for workers as a group, instead of individuals. Collective bargaining is conducted by representatives of both management and employees. The employees are represented by union members who are elected by their fellow members, or, in some cases, by professional negotiators who are employed by the union.

Labor agreements cover a wide range of areas, including wages, working conditions, health care, and retirement. For instance, labor agreements set starting wages for new employees, raises, and rules for overtime. In 2011 the United Auto Workers (UAW), the main union for automobile workers in the United States, negotiated a contract with the carmaker Ford whereby new employees would be paid $15.78 an hour, which would rise to $19.28 an hour after four years. In addition, new hires received a $6,000 signing bonus and all employees were given a minimum of $3,700 per year in profit sharing. Sometimes negotiations between one company and unions set precedents for the entire industry. In the case of the Ford talks, the resultant contract served as the basis for negotiations between unions representing auto workers and other carmakers, such as General Motors and Chrysler.

National unions oversee negotiations with large corporations and assist local unions in talks with smaller companies. Sometimes local affiliates of large unions have special groups, known as work committees, which interact with management to negotiate issues that would be specific for that branch. This could include local matters such as parking, employee cafeterias, or time off for regional holidays.

CHAPTER TWO: UNIONS AND COLLECTIVE ACTION

Fast-food workers in Tokyo on strike in 2015 to protest poor working conditions and low pay.

LABOR DISPUTES

Disputes or disagreements between unions and management are not always resolved through negotiations. In these cases, workers and owners often turn to neutral outside bodies to settle issues. For instance, the Labor Relations Agency in the United Kingdom, or the National Labor Relations Board (NLRB) in the United States, may be called in to negotiate between labor and management if the two sides are at an impasse. Unions

EMPLOYMENT AND WORKERS' RIGHTS

 PROFESSIONAL ATHLETES

Professional athletes in the United States are typically members of a union. Major league baseball players belong to the Major League Baseball Players Association (MLBPA), Football players belong to the National Football League Players Association (NFLPA), and basketball players join the National Basketball Players Association (NBPA). These unions use the same strategies and tactics of other organized labor groups. In 1994, for example, the MLBPA went on strike in opposition to an effort by team owners to install a salary cap, a limit on the amount that could be paid to an individual player. The strike lasted 232 days and resulted in the cancellation of the World Series for the first time since 1904.

or companies may also take each other to court if they believe that the other side has violated the law.

Another way to resolve disputes is through **arbitration**, which requires the two sides in disagreement to accept the recommendation of an impartial outsider. The use of arbitration to settle labor disputes has become increasingly common in Western Europe and the United States. It is generally faster and less expensive than using the courts to resolve differences.

If other forms of dispute-resolution fail, management or workers may resort to extreme measures. Workers may withhold their labor through strikes, causing companies to loss revenue. Strikers may also **picket** companies in an effort to prevent customers from frequenting the business or other workers from going to work. For their part, management may institute a **lockout**, in which employees are prohibiting from working. Lockouts mean employees are not paid, and companies use the tactic in an effort to force workers to accept their terms.

Unfortunately, as noted in the last chapter, these types of labor disputes can lead to violence. For example, after years of disputes between unions and mining companies in

CHAPTER TWO: UNIONS AND COLLECTIVE ACTION

Attempts to deregulate the labor market in France in 2006 led to widespread demonstrations, strikes, and rioting.

EMPLOYMENT AND WORKERS' RIGHTS

South Africa, a 2012 strike at a mine in the area of Marikana has become infamous as the Marikana Massacre; 34 miners were killed and 78 more wounded by police—most were shot in the back. In September 2015, police in Bengal, India, arrested more than 1,000 striking workers following riots and looting.

Text-Dependent Questions

1. Why do some business owners oppose unions?
2. What are the main differences between open-shop and closed-shop businesses?
3. Besides strikes, what other tactics might be used to settle a labor dispute?

Research Projects

1. Research organized labor, and choose a specific union. Create a timeline that presents the milestones in the creation of the union and its major achievements.
2. Research right-to-work laws. Make up your own mind about whether or not workers should be required to join a union in order to work somewhere, and then write an essay defending your view.

Chapter Three

WORKING CONDITIONS

Words to Understand

hazmat (hazardous material) suit: a whole-body protective garment that prevents contact with dangerous chemicals or biological agents.

overtime: additional pay for work beyond the maximum established workweek, usually a worker's normal salary plus 50 percent.

pension: a set amount of money regularly paid to a worker, or his or her dependents, after the employee ceases work because of retirement or disability.

workers' compensation: an insurance system whereby lost wages and medical expenses are paid to an employee who is injured while working.

EMPLOYMENT AND WORKERS' RIGHTS

Japanese commuters in the Akihabara district of downtown Tokyo.

CHAPTER THREE: WORKING CONDITIONS

In the 19th and 20th centuries, democracies enacted a wide range of new laws to protect workers and make working conditions more humane and fair. Among the most significant of these measures were rules that set the working day at 8 hours, the workweek at 40 hours, and required companies to pay **overtime** for work beyond that maximum.

While laws like these are common around the world, there is a lot of variation as to the particular details. For instance, while the United States and Japan have 40-hour workweeks, France stipulates 35 hours, while in the United Kingdom, it is 48 hours. Despite its 40-hour workweek, many Japanese prefer to work overtime, prompting the government to enact *limits* on overtime of 15 hours per week or 27 hours over a two-week period, decreasing in steps to a maximum of 120 hours over three months. In Germany almost all employees have Saturday and Sunday off, and workweeks average between 35 and 40 hours per week.

Another common worker benefit in advanced democracies is paid time off. Many nations require employers to provide a minimum number of paid vacation or sick days. For instance, Argentina requires business owners to pay wages for time off during the nation's 11 national holidays, as well as 10 personal days, for a total of 21 days. In

SHORTER WORKWEEKS

In the United States, the 40-hour workweek has been the standard for most workers since legislation was enacted in 1938. However, in Europe, a number of countries have decreased the workweek. In 2000, France cut the workweek to 35 hours, partially in an effort to get companies to hire more workers. The rationale was that if a company cut five hours per week from seven employees, they would then have to hire another worker to maintain production. In reality, most companies increased efficiency by making existing workers more productive through increased mechanization or computerization.

31

Belgium, total paid time off depends on work status: All workers get 10 paid public holidays, but if one works 6 days a week, Belgian law mandates 24 paid days off, while those who work 5 days per week get 20 days paid leave. In the United States, paid time off is left to the discretion of the individual employer; however, the 1993 Family and Medical Leave Act requires companies to grant up to 12 weeks during a single year of *unpaid* leave for personal or family illnesses, pregnancy and childbirth, and certain other family medical issues (more on this in chapter four).

Health and Safety

Democracies have enacted an increasing number of laws to protect workers and ensure their safety. These measures are designed to prevent injury or long-term disability. For example, a variety of laws restrict workers' exposure to harmful chemicals or biological agents. Consequently, most nations have strict laws about how chemicals are stored and handled, including mandates for the use of protective equipment such as gloves, goggles, and even **hazmat (hazardous material) suits**. Companies are also required to provide first-aid stations with equipment to treat accidental exposure to dangerous materials.

The risks of working with dangerous machinery are also minimized through the use of protective gear, such as goggles to prevent eye injury. The machines themselves are also required to have safety features such as emergency cut-off mechanisms or guards to prevent workers from losing fingers or limbs when they come in contact with machinery. Other types of protective equipment include hearing protection. Hearing loss is the leading long-term industrial injury in many countries, including Canada, France, and the United States.

A range of government agencies have been created to oversee worker safety. In Denmark, the Working Environment Authority (WEA) sets standards for working conditions and conducts inspections to ensure businesses are compliment. The

CHAPTER THREE: WORKING CONDITIONS

Worker in a fireproof suit.

EMPLOYMENT AND WORKERS' RIGHTS

Hearing loss is a common long-term worker injury.

CHAPTER THREE: WORKING CONDITIONS

Occupational Safety and Health Administration (OSHA) performs a similar role in the United States.

FIRE SAFETY

Fires caused some of the worst industrial accidents in history and helped spur efforts to improve worker safety. On March 25, 1911, a fire broke out at the Triangle Shirtwaist Company factory in New York. The company produced women's clothing and was located on the top three floors of a 10-story building. After the fire began, the employees, mostly young women, were unable to evacuate the building because the business owners had illegally locked most of the exits to prevent workers from taking unauthorized breaks or stealing. Although fire fighters reached the blaze fairly soon after it started, their ladders could not reach the top floors. As the flames spread, an estimated 40 women jumped to their deaths rather than burn, and 146 people were killed in the fire. Public outcry over the incident led New York to revise its workers' safety codes and to enact workers' compensation legislation. The Triangle Shirtwaist Factory Fire remains one of the deadliest industrial accidents in U.S. history.

Unfortunately, the need for stricter fire codes and worker safety regulations continues to be highlighted by horrific accidents around the world. In May 2015 a fire at a shoe factory in Manila, the Philippines, killed 72 people.

Victims of the Triangle Shirtwaist Factory Fire.

EMPLOYMENT AND WORKERS' RIGHTS

Workers' Compensation

In the past, if a worker was hurt or permanently disabled, they were not compensated and, indeed, were often fired. Often, because of their injuries, the employees would not be able to secure another job. In some countries, such as the United States or Great Britain, workers could, in theory, take business owners to court for unsafe working conditions, but such suits were seldom successful, since the wealthy and elite had enormous influence within the legal system.

In the 1800s, workers and unions began to seek compensation or **pensions** for those who were hurt on the job. Meanwhile, legislation began to offer more protection for workers. In 1880, Great Britain enacted the Employer's Liability Act, which entitled workers or their families to compensation from their employers in the event of an accident caused by supervisors or fellow workers. Three years later, Germany passed the Sickness Insurance Law, followed in 1884 by the Accident Insurance Law. These two measures created an insurance system whereby employers paid a small amount per worker into an insurance pool. If workers became sick or were injured through work, they were paid a portion of their wages until they were able to work.

These German laws became the model for modern **workers' compensation** programs. Employers pay a small percentage equal to about 1–1.5 percent of a worker's wages into an insurance program, which then compensates employees who are injured or killed on the job.

Privacy

Privacy in the workplace has become an increasingly complicated issue for workers and employers. Employers have a right to supervise their employees to ensure they are working and performing their duties as specified. However, electronic monitoring has become increasingly common, raising issues about privacy rights.

There are significant differences among democracies in terms of employee privacy rights. In the United States, companies may conduct broad background examinations

CHAPTER THREE: WORKING CONDITIONS

that include checks for a criminal record and of one's financial background, such as a credit check. In Western Europe, employees conducting background checks can only examine information that is directly related to the potential job. There are also differences on employee monitoring, including video monitoring or the examination of electronic communications. U.S. companies have much broader powers to monitor everyday activity and electronic communications, while companies in European states have more restrictions.

In the United Kingdom, there are laws that protect an employee's privacy, but the laws also give a company the right to monitor communications to ensure e-mail is not being misused. These seemingly contradictory measures have led companies to

People often assume that the e-mails they send and receive at work are private; although laws vary by country, that is usually not the case.

EMPLOYMENT AND WORKERS' RIGHTS

create very specific e-mail policies about what can and cannot be done while using a business e-mail. For instance, most companies forbid employees from visiting obscene or pornographic websites. In addition, companies may restrict workers from sites such as Facebook or Reddit to make sure employees are concentrating on their jobs.

Text-Dependent Questions

1. What were some of the most important reforms to labor laws in the 19th and 20th centuries?
2. What were the models for modern workers' compensation laws?
3. What are the main differences between employee privacy laws in the United States and Europe?

Research Projects

1. Research whether or not shorter workweeks hurt or help a nation's economy. Create a chart that compares two countries, one with a workweek of less than 40 hours, and one with a workweek of more than 40 hours. Examine factors such as gross national product, unemployment, or average income.
2. Research workers' online privacy rights. Write a paper on whether or not some or all of workers' online activity at work should be kept private from their employer.

Chapter Four

FAIRNESS IN THE WORKPLACE

Words to Understand

affirmative action: initiatives designed to compensate for past discrimination by providing additional opportunities to particular groups.

disadvantaged: an individual or group of people that lack the same economic, educational, and social opportunities as others in a society.

glass ceiling: obstacles that prevent the advancement of disadvantaged groups from obtaining senior positions of authority in business, government, and education.

sexual harassment: unwelcome verbal or physical sexual advances, or other unacceptable conduct of a sexual nature, in the workplace or other professional setting.

EMPLOYMENT AND WORKERS' RIGHTS

In addition to the broad effort to make the workplace safer over the last two centuries, there have also been successive campaigns to make it fairer. Democracies have passed a number of laws to eliminate discrimination based on factors such as race, gender, or religion. In addition, democracies have endeavored to make the workplace accommodating for people with disabilities.

In some cases, efforts to ensure workplace equality have resulted in programs designed to increase the number of **disadvantaged** groups in the workplace. In other instances, governments have endeavored to reduce or end disparities in pay among workers based on factors such as race or gender. The result has been more inclusive workplaces and less overt discrimination.

Discrimination

Discrimination in the workplace can be subtle and comes in many forms. For instance, bias may result in a manager not hiring people of certain races even if they are more qualified than other applicants. Discrimination issues may also arise when older employees lose their jobs; older employees have often been at a company longer than their younger counterparts, and therefore make more money. Discrimination may also mean that certain groups are not promoted as fast as others. For instance, in the United Kingdom in 2015, a black police officer, Ronnie Lungu, won a discrimination case against the Wiltshire Police Force for repeatedly passing him over for promotion, despite high scores on his sergeant's exam.

Sexual harassment is another form of workplace discrimination. Countries have increasingly sought to reduce sexual harassment by increasing awareness of the problem and increasing fines and punishments. In France, individuals and employers found guilty of sexual harassment are subject to a $31,000 fine per occurrence, and up to a two-year jail sentence. Civil fines for sexual harassment can be even greater. In 2011, in the United States, a jury awarded Ashley Alford $95 million in a suit against Aaron's Inc. for a case of extreme sexual harassment that lasted more than a year (the award was later reduced to about $40 million).

CHAPTER FOUR: FAIRNESS IN THE WORKPLACE

Many democracies have laws in place that prohibit discrimination in hiring based on gender or ethnicity. A few also prohibit discrimination by sexuality or gender identity, but those are much less common.

Efforts to Prevent Discrimination

Most democracies, including Australia, Canada, Japan, the United States, and the nations of Western Europe, have various laws in place that forbid discrimination in hiring and employment based on a range of factors, including disability, ethnicity, gender, race, religion, sexual orientation, and age. In the United States, Title VII of the 1964 Civil Rights Act is the cornerstone of regulation to prohibit discrimination, along with subsequent legislation and revisions such as the 1967 Age Discrimination in Employment

EMPLOYMENT AND WORKERS' RIGHTS

President Lyndon Johnson signs the 1964 Civil Rights Act.

Act and the 1990 Americans with Disabilities Act. There is no federal measure in the United States that bans discrimination based on sexual identity, although about half of U.S. states do have anti-bias laws in place.

Governments have created various agencies in order to enforce antidiscrimination measures. In Australia, the Australian Human Rights Commission and the Fair Work Ombudsman oversee enforcement of antidiscrimination legislation and conduct investigations at the national level, while each of Australia's six states has its own commission on fair labor practices. In most democracies, employers who engage in discrimination can be held liable on both criminal and civil levels. This means that the government can fine or otherwise punish the company, while the employee or groups that suffered discrimination can sue the business for compensation.

CHAPTER FOUR: FAIRNESS IN THE WORKPLACE

MILITARY DISCRIMINATION

The military remains one area in which countries permit open discrimination because of the nature of its activities, including extreme physical training and missions. The result is that the armed forces have various restrictions on height, weight, and educational attainment. Militaries also ban people with various disabilities, and they also have fairly rigid age restrictions. While the military has traditionally been dominated by men, countries have expanded the role of women within their armed services.

The most significant change has been reforms that allow women to serve in combat units. Countries such as New Zealand and Sweden allow women in all branches and units of the military, while other nations, such as the United Kingdom and Spain, continue to have restrictions on women in combat. The United States removed a formal ban on women in combat units in 2013, although some restrictions continue.

In 2011, American soldiers took part in a panel discussion on "Women Serving in Combat" at Camp Liberty, in Iraq.

EMPLOYMENT AND WORKERS' RIGHTS

Employment Equality

Disadvantaged groups, such as racial minorities or women, do not have the same opportunities as others, and antidiscrimination measures alone have not been enough to dramatically increase prospects for these populations. Furthermore, some forms of employment discrimination are difficult to detect, especially issues such as promotion. Women and other disadvantaged groups often face a **glass ceiling** in their efforts to rise to positions of authority. For example, the *Economist* reported in 2005 that of the United Kingdom's largest companies, women led only 17, while men were in charge of more than 400. At the time, women only led 5 percent of France's major companies and 8 percent of major U.S. firms.

In response to these inequities, many governments have implemented **affirmative action** (also known as employment equality) programs. Affirmative action programs have been implemented differently in different countries. For instance, in Canada the emphasis is on proactive efforts to recruit from disadvantaged groups. Companies are encouraged to advertise for open jobs in the languages of groups such as indigenous people or immigrant communities. They may also undertake special recruitment fairs in

CONTROVERSY OVER AFFIRMATIVE ACTION

Not all nations use extensive affirmative action or employment equality programs. Opponents of these programs assert that they unfairly discriminate against non-disadvantaged groups by using racial, gender, religious, or other preferences. For instance, there are no formal affirmative action programs in hiring or promotion in the United Kingdom, although companies may hire or promote underrepresented groups in cases where two or more finalists for a job are equal in qualifications and potential. In the United States, affirmative action programs are controversial. Eight U.S. states have banned affirmative action in college admissions.

CHAPTER FOUR: FAIRNESS IN THE WORKPLACE

PARENTAL LEAVE

In the past, pregnancy was a common reason for women to leave the workforce, either voluntarily or forcibly. In the 20th century, however, countries began enacting new rules to give women, and increasingly men, parental leave—time off before or after the birth of a child. European nations typically have the most generous parental leave. In Estonia, for instance, women may take up to 62 weeks off after childbirth, with 100 percent of their salary. The United Kingdom allows 52 weeks at 90 percent salary. Finland allows women 18 weeks at 70 percent salary, but also permits men to take 11 weeks off at 70 percent (Iceland allows men 12 week at 80 percent pay, but women only receive 13 weeks off at 80 percent). Time off may begin before the birth of a child; Germany allows expectant mothers to take leave up to 6 weeks before the expected due date of a child.

Japan permits women 14 weeks at 60 percent salary, but it also allows up to a year unpaid time off (there is no paid or unpaid parental leave for men). The United States is an outlier among developed democracies in that there is no national requirement for paid time off for either men or women following childbirth. Americans are permitted up to 12 weeks of unpaid leave. (For more on family leave policies, see the volume *Gender Equality and Identity Rights* in this set.)

disadvantaged communities or provide additional training or apprenticeship programs for these groups. Other countries are more specific. Norway requires that women make up at least 40 percent of the corporate boards for public companies.

WAGES

Wages are a major area of contention in workplace fairness. One of the objectives of antidiscrimination measures has been to ensure that workers receive equal pay for

EMPLOYMENT AND WORKERS' RIGHTS

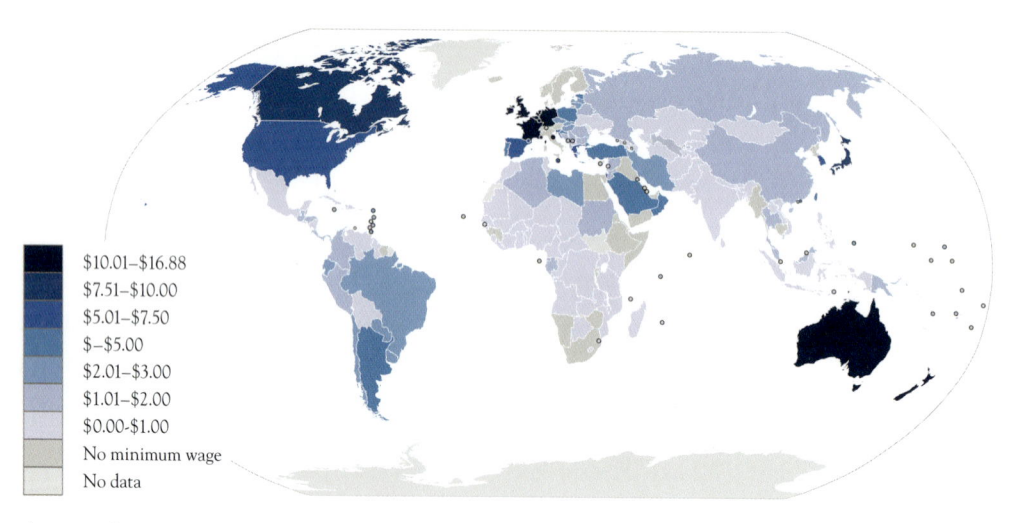

A map of minimum wages in U.S. dollars, as of 2014.

equal work. However, even among nations with strong antidiscrimination laws, there continue to be significant gaps between workers. This is most pronounced in the wage disparity between men and women, known as the "gender gap." Even in most wealthy democracies, women usually only make about 75–80 percent of the salary of men. Some of the difference is explained by the different occupations often chosen by men and women (including full-time versus part-time work), and by cultural factors such as responsibility for child rearing and the potential time that takes away from one's career. However, studies have consistently shown that discrimination continues to be a significant factor in the difference.

The minimum wage is an area of controversy in discussions on workplace fairness. Some argue that a minimum wage reduces employment by forcing employers to pay more than they otherwise would. Proponents of the minimum wage assert that it reduces worker exploitation and allows governments to set a basic standard salary. Not all wealthy, democratic nations have a minimum wage. Countries such as Austria, Denmark, Italy, and Switzerland do not have formal minimum wages. Meanwhile, in nations such as Denmark, Finland, Sweden, and Norway, unions or worker groups negotiate minimum salaries directly with employers, and there is also no national minimum wage.

CHAPTER FOUR: FAIRNESS IN THE WORKPLACE

There is wide variation among countries with minimum wages. In 2015, in the United States, the minimum wage was $7.25 an hour ($15,080 per year), although some localities have raised it as high as $15 an hour ($31,200). That year, in the United Kingdom, it was £6.70 (around $10) per hour for workers 21 and older, £5.30 (around $8) for those 18–20, and £3.87 (just under $6) for those under 18. In Canada, there is no national minimum wage; instead, each province sets its own, ranging in 2015 from $10.30 Canadian (about US$7.70) in New Brunswick to $11.25 Canadian (about US$8.40) in Ontario.

Text Dependent Questions

1. What are some forms of workplace discrimination?
2. What are affirmative action programs designed to accomplish?
3. What are the causes of the gender gap?

Research Projects

1. Research workplace discrimination. Choose a specific case of workplace discrimination and write a report that explains what happened and what steps were taken in response?
2. Research minimum wage laws. Write a report on whether or not the minimum wage helps the economy.

Chapter Five

Termination

Words to Understand

class action lawsuit: group legal action in which individuals band together to sue over a perceived wrong.

downsize: to make a company's staff smaller by permanently eliminating positions.

layoff: the suspension, or termination, of workers caused through no fault of the employee; usually temporary.

severance package: a payment or other benefits given to an employee when he or she leaves a business; it is typically based on a formula that gives a worker more money the longer he or she has worked for the company.

One of the most powerful tools of employers is the ability to dismiss or fire an employee. In the past, workers could be terminated for almost any cause. New rules and regulations adopted in the 19th and 20th centuries provided increasing protections for workers from being fired. Some of these measures included prohibitions against discrimination, while others offered recourse for those dismissed without proper cause.

CHAPTER FIVE: TERMINATION

Layoffs

Unfortunately, some businesses have to lay off workers from time to time. Companies may have busy seasons when they need more workers because of increased demand or production of products. The firms hire additional workers, but then lay them off when demand falls, hiring them again when needed. Countries define these temporary **layoffs** as lasting for a set period of time, which is preplanned. For instance, in Ontario, Canada, a temporary layoff consists of not more than 13 weeks in any given 20-week period.

Layoffs can impact a small portion of employees or very large groups of workers.

EMPLOYMENT AND WORKERS' RIGHTS

WRONGFUL TERMINATION

People who are dismissed for unlawful reasons usually have two ways to respond. First, the fired worker can file a complaint with the government office that oversees workers' rights. Second, an employee can file a lawsuit against the company.

In some cases, a number of employees that have been wronged join together in what is known as a **class action lawsuit**, in which they sue as a group. In 2009, for example, six former Walmart workers filed a lawsuit against the company for wrongful termination. The six were fired for completing an employee satisfaction survey more than once. Walmart settled the suit out of court.

During temporary layoffs, workers may continue to receive reduced pay from the employer and maintain benefits such as health insurance.

Layoffs may also be permanent. Companies may permanently **downsize** their workforce when sales or demand decline. For example, the U.S. carmaker General Motors eliminated more than 47,000 positions, beginning in February 2009, in response to the Great Recession. While companies are usually free to eliminate positions, some countries, such as Germany, require approval from the government before a firm can eliminate a significant portion of its workforce during a one-month period.

France requires companies to create a jobs plan when a corporation intends to lay off more than 10 employees during a one-month period. Among other things, the plan must explain steps taken to preserve jobs and detail a **severance package**. Companies must wait at least 30 days in layoffs of up to 100 employees, 45 days for layoffs of 100–249 workers, and 60 days for more than 250 employees. This gives workers time to find other employment. During large layoffs, French law requires severance packages equal to one-fifth of a workers monthly salary for each year worked up to 10 years. Employees with more than 10 years of service receive packages equal to one-third of their monthly pay for each additional year beyond the 10.

CHAPTER FIVE: TERMINATION

Termination and Unemployment

Workers can be fired for a variety of legitimate reasons. They can be terminated for infractions such as theft, fraud, or insubordination. They may be dismissed for business reasons; for example, if the corporation closes down a branch or division. However, employment law in most countries is designed to prevent workers from being fired unfairly. For instance, a number of nations, including Germany, require employers to give employees written notification if they are being dismissed. In addition, German

Unemployed people waiting in line at a government employment office in Madrid, Spain.

EMPLOYMENT AND WORKERS' RIGHTS

MIGRANT WORKERS

In many countries, temporary workers do not have the same rights as full-time employees. They may be fired more easily and generally do not have the same rights or benefits as full-time staff. Workers who are not citizens may face even more challenges. For instance, unscrupulous employers might use the threat of deportation to pay undocumented workers substandard wages (or they might not pay them at all). Even legal migrant workers often face challenges in terms of poor or unsafe working conditions and substandard wages.

In response, the United Nations sponsored the 1990 International Convention on the Protection of the Rights of All Migrant Workers and Members of Their Families. However, only 48 countries have ratified the agreement. The United States and the nations of Western Europe have not signed the agreement.

Seasonal farmworkers pick strawberries in Salinas, California. Migrant workers do not have the same protections that other types of workers do, and they often work under difficult conditions.

CHAPTER FIVE: TERMINATION

law states that workers who have been with a company for more than six months can only be fired for a series of specific reasons, including misconduct, long-term sick leave, or business factors.

People who lose their jobs may be eligible for unemployment benefits, including cash payments. Unemployment benefits vary from country to country. In the United States, the individual states oversee unemployment benefits. Companies pay a small tax on each employee, which goes into a fund. Employees who become unemployed can receive payments for six months. The payments vary depending on the state; they are a percentage of a worker's income up to a maximum amount. For instance, in 2015, Alabama paid a minimum of $45 per week, up to a maximum of $265 per week, while Massachusetts paid a weekly minimum of $33, up to a maximum of $1,101.

Many other countries take a different approach. Unemployed workers in Australia and most European countries do not have limits on the amount of time they receive unemployment benefits as long as they abide by certain rules. For instance, to remain eligible for benefits, the unemployed typically have to be actively searching for a job or enrolled in worker training programs. In these countries, unemployment benefits are paid by the national government from general taxes, not employer contributions.

Pensions

Workers leave the workforce through retirement at the end of their working life. Efforts to provide support for retired workers have led to the creation of often complex **pension** system in democracies, in which retirees receive payments and benefits from either their former employers or the government (or both). In Norway, all citizens receive a pension from the state at age 67. In 2013, that pension was worth about $2,325 per month. In addition, all working Norwegians are covered by either a private pension plan through the company at which they work, or a state plan in which the employee contributes a minimum of 2 percent of a worker's annual salary.

EMPLOYMENT AND WORKERS' RIGHTS

In 2015, union members went on strike in Halifax, Nova Scotia, to resist proposed changes to their pension plan.

Several nations, including Canada and the United States, have retirement systems in which the worker and the employer annually contribute a percentage of the worker's salary to the national pension plan. In Canada, the worker and the employer each contribute 4.95 percent of salary (total of 9.9 percent), while in the United States, the figure is 6.2 percent (total of 12.4 percent). When workers reach retirement age, they are eligible for monthly payments that are based on how much they contributed over their working lives. Canada and the United States also provide incentives for workers that retire later. For example, in the United States, if a worker retires at age 70, instead of 65, his or her monthly payment increases noticeably.

CHAPTER FIVE: TERMINATION

PENSION BURDENS

In many developed countries, the number of people who are retired has grown dramatically, which has created a growing strain on government budgets. For instance, in 2012 there were 4.2 workers for every retiree in France, but by 2050 that number is expected to decline to 1.9 workers for every pensioner. This means less money in taxes or contributions to fund retirement systems. In the United States, Social Security had a $39 billion deficit in 2014. Officials reported the pension and disability system would go bankrupt in 2035, forcing across-the-board cuts of at least 23 percent in the program.

In Paris, protesters object to attempts at pension reform, 2010.

EMPLOYMENT AND WORKERS' RIGHTS

Pensions ensure that workers have some means of support after they retire. The programs also form an important part of the broader series of workers' rights in democracies. Collectively, these rights have enhanced the safety and security of modern workers, and they have reduced unfairness, including discrimination, in the workplace. However, challenges remain, especially in areas such as diversity in the workplace.

Text-Dependent Questions

1. What are some reasons that companies lay off workers?
2. What are unemployment benefits?
3. How do countries such as the United States and Canada fund their pension systems?

Research Projects

1. Research unemployment benefits in a democratic country of your choice. Write a report that examines how unemployment benefits are similar to, or different from, those of the United States.
2. Research pension systems. Write a report that explores why countries want workers to retire later in life. What benefits does the nation receive, and what benefits does the worker gain?

FURTHER READING

Books

Dray, Philip. *There Is Power in a Union: The Epic Story of Labor in America.* New York: Doubleday, 2010.

Fernie, Sue, and David Mecalf, eds. *Trade Unions: Resurgence or Demise?* New York: Routledge, 2005.

Gross, James A. Ed. *Workers' Rights as Human Rights.* Ithaca, NY: Cornell University Press, 2003.

Painter, Richard W., and Keith Puttick, with Ann Holmes. *Employment Rights.* 3rd ed. Ann Arbor: Pluto Press, 2004.

Online

Human Rights Watch. https://www.hrw.org/.
International Labour Organization. http://www.ilo.org/global/lang--en/index.htm.
United States Department of Labor. http://www.dol.gov/.
World Trade Organization. https://www.wto.org/.

SERIES GLOSSARY

accountability: making elected officials and government workers answerable to the public for their actions, and holding them responsible for mistakes or crimes.

amnesty: a formal reprieve or pardon for people accused or convicted of committing crimes.

anarchist: a person who believes that government should be abolished because it enslaves or otherwise represses people.

assimilation: the process through which immigrants adopt the cultural, political, and social beliefs of a new nation.

autocracy: a system of government in which a small circle of elites holds most, if not all, political power.

belief: an acceptance of a statement or idea concerning a religion or faith.

citizenship: formal recognition that an individual is a member of a political community.

civil law: statutes and rules that govern private rights and responsibilities and regulate noncriminal disputes over issues such as property or contracts.

civil rights: government-protected liberties afforded to all people in democratic countries.

civil servants: people who work for the government, not including elected officials or members of the military.

corruption: illegal or unethical behavior on the part of officials who abuse their position.

democracy: A government in which the people hold all or most political power and express their preferences on issues through regular voting and elections.

deportation: the legal process whereby undocumented immigrants or those who have violated residency laws are forced to leave their new country.

dual citizenship: being a full citizen of two or more countries.

election: the process of selecting people to serve in public office through voting.

expatriate: someone who resides in a country other than his or her nation of birth.

feminism: the belief in social, economic, and political equality for women.

gender rights: providing access to equal rights for all members of a society regardless of their gender.

glass ceiling: obstacles that prevent the advancement of disadvantaged groups from obtaining senior positions of authority in business, government, and education.

globalization: a trend toward increased interconnectedness between nations and cultures across the world; globalization impacts the spheres of politics, economics, culture, and mass media.

guest workers: citizens of one country who have been granted permission to temporarily work in another nation.

SERIES GLOSSARY

homogenous: a region or nation where most people have the same ethnicity, language, religion, customs, and traditions.

human rights: rights that everyone has, regardless of birthplace or citizenship.

incumbent: an official who currently holds office.

industrialization: the transformation of social life resulting from the technological and economic developments involving factories.

jurisdiction: the official authority to administer justice through activities such as investigations, arrests, and obtaining testimony.

minority: a group that is different—ethnically, racially, culturally, or in terms of religion—within a larger society.

national security: the combined efforts of a country to protect its citizens and interests from harm.

naturalization: the legal process by which a resident noncitizen becomes a citizen of a country.

nongovernmental organization (NGO): a private, nonprofit group that provides services or attempts to influence governments and international organizations.

oligarchy: a country in which political power is held by a small, powerful, but unelected group of leaders.

partisanship: a strong bias or prejudice toward one set of beliefs that often results in an unwillingness to compromise or accept alternative points of view.

refugees: people who are kicked out of their country or forced to flee to another country because they are not welcome or fear for their lives.

right-to-work laws: laws in the United States that forbid making union membership a condition for employment.

secular state: governments that are not officially influenced by religion in making decisions.

sexism: system of beliefs, or ideology, that asserts the inferiority of one sex and justifies discrimination based on gender.

socialist: describes a political system in which major businesses or industries are owned or regulated by the community instead of by individuals or privately owned companies.

socioeconomic status: the position of a person within society, based on the combination of their income, wealth, education, family background, and social standing.

sovereignty: supreme authority over people and geographic space. National governments have sovereignty over their citizens and territory.

theocracy: a system of government in which all major decisions are made under the guidance of religious leaders' interpretation of divine authority.

treason: the betrayal of one's country.

tyranny: rule by a small group or single person.

veto: the ability to reject a law or other measure enacted by a legislature.

wage gap: the disparity in earnings between men and women for their work.

INDEX

A
Aaron's Inc., 40
Accident Insurance Law, 36
activists, 14
affirmative action, 39, 44
Age Discrimination in
 Employment Act, 41–42
agreements, 24
agriculture, 10
Alabama, 53
Alford, Ashley, 40
All-China Federation
 of Trade Unions
 (ACFTU), 21
Amalgamated Transit Union
 in New York, 23
Americans with Disabilities
 Act, 42
anarchists, 9, 14
antidiscrimination, 42, 44,
 45–46
antigovernment movements,
 17
apprenticeships, 10
arbitration, 19, 26
Argentina, 31
artisans, 10
athletes, 26
Australia, 13, 14, 16, 24, 41,
 42, 53
Australian Human Rights
 Commission, 42
Austria, 46
auto workers, 24

B
baseball, 26
basketball, 26
Battle of the Viaduct, 13
Belgium, 32
benefits, 21, 53
Bengal, India, 28
bombs, 13
bribes, 23
businesses
 closed and open shops, 23
 laws for, 31–32, 36
 layoffs and, 48, 50
 pickets at, 26
 strikes against, 11
 and unions, 21–23
 unsafe working conditions
 in, 36

C
Canada, 32, 41, 44, 47, 54
chemicals, 14, 32
children, 11, 14, 45
China, 20, 21
Chrysler, 24
Civil Rights Act of 1964, 41
class action lawsuits, 48, 50
closed and open shops, 23–24
collective bargaining, 19, 24
colonies, 13
Combination Acts in 1799
 and 1800, 11
communications, 12, 37
conspiracy, 14

contracts, 23, 24
corruption, 21, 23
Cuba, 20

D
democracies, 42
 fairness efforts in, 40, 41
 gender gap in, 46
 health and safety in, 32–35
 pension systems in, 53
 privacy in, 36–38
 unions in, 21–22
 working conditions in, 31
demonstrations, 13, 17, 27
Denmark, 32, 46
Department of Labor, 23
disabilities
 accommodations, 40
 compensation for, 36
 discrimination, 41
 and the military, 43
 prevention of, 32
disadvantaged groups, 39,
 40, 44
discrimination, 40–43
disputes, 13, 25–26, 28
downsizing, 48, 50
dues, 23, 24

E
Economist, 44
8-hour workday, 14
electronic monitoring, 36–37
e-mail privacy, 37–38

INDEX

employees, 11
   and contract negotiations, 24
   dismissing, 48
   equality for, 44–45
   older, 40
   privacy of, 36–37
   and union formation, 22
employers, 11, 13, 18, 42
   see also businesses
Employer's Liability Act, 36
employment rights, 11
equality, 40, 44–45
equal pay for equal work, 46
Estonia, 45
ethnicity, 41
Europe, 10, 13, 45, 53

F

factories, 11, 14
fairness in the workplace, 39–48
   defined, 39–40
   discrimination, 40–43
   and employment equality, 44–45
   and wages, 45–47
Fair Work Ombudsman, 42
Family and Medical Leave Act, 32
Finland, 45, 46
fire safety, 35
First International (International Workingman's Association), 17
football, 26
Ford, 24

Frame Breaking Act of 1812, 13
France
   affirmative action in, 44
   hearing loss in, 32
   hours of work in, 14, 31
   layoffs in, 50
   pensions in, 55
   political parties in, 17
   reforms in, 14
   sexual harassment in, 40

G

gender, 40, 41
gender gap, 46
General Motors, 24, 50
Germany, 17, 31, 36, 45, 50, 53
glass ceiling, 39, 44
government agencies, 32, 34–35
Great Britain, 11–13, 18, 36
Great Recession, 50
guilds, 10

H

Hayes, Rutherford B., 13
Haymarket Riot, 13, 14
hazmat (hazardous material) suit, 29, 32
health and safety, 24, 32–35
hearing loss, 32
holidays, labor, 14, 31–32
hours, 14, 31–32
hygiene standards, 14

I

India, 22

industrialization, 13
Industrial Revolution, 9, 10, 11, 12
injuries, 11
insurance systems, 36
International Convention on the Protection of the Rights of All Migrant Workers and Members of Their Families, 52
International Workingman's Association (First International), 17
inventions, 12
Italy, 46

J

Japan, 31, 41, 45

L

labor
   child, 14
   disputes, 25–26, 28
   holidays, 14
   organized, 20
   reforms, 14, 16, 18
   unrest, 13–14
labor board, 19, 22
Labor Relations Agency in the United Kingdom, 25
Labour Party, 18
laws
   anti-bias, 42
   health and safety, 32
   right-to-work, 23–24
   against strikes, 11
   termination, 48
   wage, 18

EMPLOYMENT AND WORKERS' RIGHTS

worker protection, 31
workers' compensation, 36
wrongful termination, 50
layoffs, 48–50
leave, 32
lockouts, 19, 26
Luddites, 13
Lungu, Ronnie, 40
Lyon, 13

M

machines, 12, 13, 32
Major League Baseball Players Association (MLBPA), 26
Manila, Philippines, 35
manufacturing, 12, 14
Marikana Massacre, 28
Massachusetts, 53
May Day, 14
memberships, 10, 22
migrant workers, 52
military discrimination, 43
miners, 14, 28
minimum wages, 16–17, 46

N

National Basketball Players Association (NBPA), 26
National Football League Players Association (NFLPA), 26
National Labor Relations Board (NLRB), 25
negotiations, 24
negotiators, 24
Newcomen, Thomas, 12
New Zealand, 16–17, 24, 43

North America, 12
Norway, 45, 46, 53

O

Occupational Safety and Health Administration (OSHA), 34
older employees, 40
Ontario, Canada, 49
open and closed shops, 23–24
overtime, 24, 29, 31

P

parental leave, 45
Parliament, 18
pensions, 29, 36, 53–56
persecution, 20
picket, 19, 26
pledge cards, 22
police, 13, 14
politics, 18, 21, 23
population increase, 11
pregnancy, 45
prices, 10
prisons, 13
privacy, 36–38
private ownership, 17
professional societies, 10
profit sharing, 24
promotions, 40, 44
protective equipment, 32
protests, 13
punishments, 13

R

race, 40–43
railroads, 13
raises, 24

recruitment, 44–45
reforms, 14, 16, 17–18
religion, 40, 41
representation, 24
retirement, 24, 53–56, 54
revolutions, 13
rights of workers, 9–18
    defined, 9–11
    Industrial Revolution and, 11–12
    and labor unrest, 13–14
    reforms for, 14, 16, 18
right-to-work laws, 19, 21–24, 23–24
riots, 13
Russia, 17

S

safety, 12, 14
    see also health and safety
Saudi Arabia, 20
severance packages, 48, 50
sexual harassment, 39, 40
sexual orientation, 41, 42
sick days, 31–32
Sickness Insurance Law, 36
socialists, 9, 18
Social Security, 55
Spain, 43
spinning jenny, 12
steam engine, 12
strikes, 9, 11, 21, 26
suppression, 20
Sweden, 43, 46
Switzerland, 46

T

technologies, 12, 13

INDEX

telegraph, 12
termination, 48–56
    defined, 48
    layoffs, 48–50
    pensions and, 53–56
    and unemployment, 51, 53
    wrongful, 50
textile workers, 13
time off, 31
trade unions, 9, 11
training, 10
transportation, 9, 12, 13
Triangle Shirtwaist Company, 35

U

UAW (United Auto Workers), 24
unemployment, 51, 53
unions, 11
    athletes and, 26
    bans on, 20
    corruption in, 21, 23
    in democracies, 21
    formation of, 21–24
    and right-to-work laws, 21–24
unions and collective action, 19–28
    and bargaining, 24
    defined, 19–21
    and labor disputes, 25–27
    right-to-work laws and, 21–24
union shops, 24
United Auto Workers (UAW), 24

United Kingdom
    affirmative action in, 44
    closed shops in, 24
    discrimination prevention in, 40
    labor relations, 25
    military women in, 43
    parental leave in, 45
    privacy rights in, 37
    wages in, 47
    women leaders in, 44
    working hours in, 31
United Nations, 52
United States
    arbitration in, 26
    discrimination prevention in, 41–42
    industrial injury prevention in, 32, 35
    migrant workers in, 52
    parental leave in, 45
    pension plans in, 54, 55
    privacy rights in, 36–37
    right-to-work laws in, 23
    strikes in, 13
    unemployment benefits in, 53
    wages in, 16, 18, 47
    women in, 43, 44
    workers' compensation in, 36
    working hours in, 14, 31
unpaid leave, 32
unrest, labor, 13–14

V

vacations, 31
violence, 13, 14, 26, 28

W

wages
    deductions from, 11
    fair, 45–47
    guilds, 10
    loss of, 13
    minimum, 16–17, 46
    setting, 24
    for times off, 31–32
Walmart, 50
Watt, James, 12
weavers, 13
Western Europe, 12, 26, 37, 41, 52
Wiltshire Police Force, 40
women, 11, 43, 44–45
work committees, 24
workers' compensation, 29, 36
working conditions, 29–38
    business owners and, 21–22
    collective bargaining and, 24
    compensation for workers, 35–36
    defined, 29, 31–32
    guilds and, 10
    health and safety, 32–35
    of the Industrial Revolution, 11–12
    privacy and, 36–38
    under Socialism, 17
Working Environment Authority (WEA), 32
wrongful termination, 50

ABOUT THE AUTHOR

Jack Covarubias currently works in the Refugee, Asylum and International Operations Directorate in the Department of Homeland Security. He is the former Director of the Center for Policy and Resilience and Assistant Professor of Political Science at The University of Southern Mississippi. His experience bridges academia and the military where he has focused on the American foreign policy experience and homeland security. His most recent works include the edited volume *The New Islamic State: Ideology, Religion and Violent Extremism in the 21st Century* (2016) and the edited volume *Culture, Rhetoric and Voting: The Presidential Election of 2012* (2015).

ABOUT THE ADVISOR

Tom Lansford is a Professor of Political Science, and a former academic dean, at the University of Southern Mississippi, Gulf Coast. He is a member of the governing board of the National Social Science Association and a state liaison for Mississippi for Project Vote Smart. His research interests include foreign and security policy, and the U.S. presidency. Dr. Lansford is the author, coauthor, editor or coeditor of more than 40 books, and the author of more than one hundred essays, book chapters, encyclopedic entries, and reviews. Recent sole-authored books include: *A Bitter Harvest: U.S. Foreign Policy and Afghanistan* (2003), the *Historical Dictionary of U.S. Diplomacy Since the Cold War* (2007) and *9/11 and the Wars in Afghanistan and Iraq: A Chronology and Reference Guide* (2011). His more recent edited collections include: *America's War on Terror* (2003; second edition 2009), *Judging Bush* (2009), and *The Obama Presidency: A Preliminary Assessment* (2012). Dr. Lansford has served as the editor of the annual *Political Handbook of the World* since 2012.

PHOTO CREDITS

Cover: iStock.com/JESP62; iStock.com/FireAtDusk; iStock.com/rightdx
iStock.com: 12 ilbusca; 25 Electra-K-Vasileiadou; 27 titoslack; 30 fotoVoyager; 33 Savas Keskiner; 34 linephone; 37 Yuri Arcurs; 41 XiXinXing; 49 Steve Debenport; 51 EdStock; 52 rightdx; 54 shaunl
National Archives and Records Administration: 22
Shutterstock: 17 Christopher Ellwell
Wikimedia Commons: 6 Al Jazeera English; 10; 15; 16; 20; 35; 42; 43; 46; 55 Myrabella

11-21-16